THE
TINY ASTRONAUT

THE TINY ASTRONAUT

Amlaan Akshayanshu Sahoo

BLACK EAGLE BOOKS
2020

BLACK EAGLE BOOKS
USA address:
7464 Wisdom Lane
Dublin, OH 43016

India address:
E/312, Trident Galaxy, Kalinga Nagar,
Bhubaneswar-751003, Odisha, India

E-mail: info@blackeaglebooks.org
Website: www.blackeaglebooks.org

First International Edition Published by
BLACK EAGLE BOOKS, 2020

THE TINY ASTRONAUT
by **Amlaan Akshayanshu Sahoo**

Copyright © **Amlaan Akshayanshu Sahoo**

All rights reserved. No part of this publication may be reproduced, stored in a retrieval system, or transmitted, in any form or by any means, electronic, mechanical, photocopying, recording or otherwise without the prior permission of the publisher.

Cover: **Dr. Dinabandhu Sahoo**
Interior Design: Ezy's Publication

ISBN- 978-1-64560-105-0 (Paperback)
Library of Congress Control Number: 2020943485

Printed in United States of America

"I do not know what I may appear to the world, but to myself I seem to have been only like a boy playing on the seashore, and diverting myself in now and then finding a smoother pebble or a prettier shell than ordinary, whilst the great ocean of truth lay all undiscovered before me."

― *Isaac Newton*

to
my
waning
childhood

this book is

a hopeful song of voices new
yet ancient in their inspiration

a bold stroke of colors different
yet confident in their adoption

stringing together poems
born of ripples
on the lake of life

evoking the
subtle complexity
unabashed versatility
blemished beauty
of being
human.

AUTHOR'S NOTE

What stirs in our hearts in the solemn moments of the night, that coaxes us to shut our eyes and enter the world of dreams, so vivid and lifelike one second, yet meaningless in the next?

What makes us see faces in clouds- feathery fantasies that are best left unshared? What stretches our lips into smiles, and what droops our eyelids as we shed precious drops of our soul, and yet keep walking on the path of life with silent, steady steps?

What is the miracle that makes us human?

These questions, and countless others, are the ones that wake me up each morning. They tug at my heart strings, whisper in my ears, waft in the winter breeze before my eyes, and sometimes...sometimes they spill out of a longing pen, taking the shape of letters, demanding answers on a white sheet in the form of a poem.

Be it nature, objects, human sentiments, or everyday affairs, there often arises a gripping wave of rumination, introspection and eye-opening enlightenment that leaves us dazed. It is this wave that some resist resiliently, while others choose to be swept away in its cold yet warm currents to the unseen extents of discovery. I, as a human, cherish and wait longingly for such moments, for they mould my still-inadequate understanding of this universe.

What they leave behind is a poem.

On the pages of this book, I have slit and spilt my heart and soul- scarred and ennobled by time, reproached by reason and rationality. I have laid bare my innermost thoughts and now wait in the thunderous quiet of expectation for response.

What will you find in here? An escape from reality? An outlet for emotions? Or the idiotic babbles of a deranged teenager? For they are mind-bending, poems- sometimes misleading too!

But whatever you seek, and whatever you see, I humbly hope that it lingers in the corridors of your imagination like the aftertaste of a new dish, however bittersweet the decision to try it might have been.

I am after all a fledgling, wonderstruck by this world, yet terrified of flying in the open sky.

This fledgling has taken his first leap, and his temerity has touched the frontiers of his earthly abode. This tiny astronaut who knows nothing of black holes, comets or gamma ray bursts, has set our sailing into the void of space. His spaceship is his thoughts, his fuel is imagination. Ink is his oxygen, blank paper his artificial gravity. Poems are his hope to live and survive. But you, kind reader, are his desire for safe homeward return.

May my unskilled attempts tempt you to explore and rediscover yourselves and others around you.

May they remind you of the welcoming doors of humanity, so that mankind does not drift too far from its threshold.

As you shut this book, may you find your curiosity aroused and your conscience enlivened, so that we all may accept and embrace the keen, sprightly child who hides in the deepest crevice of our hearts.

And what else can that child be, but a tiny astronaut!

THE
TINY ASTRONAUT

I think,
    if I will be an astronaut,
I will surely go
    to space.

But
    now that
I am so small, I think,
    I should ask
    my mom
    to tie my lace…

IN HONOUR OF WORDS

I am immensely delighted to extend my felicitation to Mr. Amlaan Akshayanshu Sahoo the budding young poet for publishing his poetry collection "THE TINY ASTRONAUT". This collection has richly expressed his imagination, visualisation, mood, feeling, and attitude to life.

The great poet Robert Frost has aptly written "*Poetry is when an emotion has found its thought and thought has found words*". So Amlaan's poetry being blended with emotion and thought communicates to the readers spontaneously with his impecable word play. He has built up an awesome work of words by his magical imagination, visualisation and awakening ability of expression. In some of his poems he has beautifully handled the theme and style with the touch of divine sublimity. Exquisite poetic upliftment with an assured creativity in his creative journey is evident. As Mr. Amlaan is a tiny astronaut of poetic world many more maturity, novelties and nuances of expression as well as profound richness of thought in his journey of words are to come up.

Still I hope his expression would enrich one's heart. Also I pray to Almighty, let his raw and intense thoughts and ability get the wings to soar high.

Satya Pattnaik
Poet

CONTENTS

Stargaze	19
Through Young Eyes	21
Window	24
His Inspiring Endeavours	26
Invigorated Aspirations	28
Countryside	29
The Moonflower's Smile	30
Blind	31
Barren	32
Inside	34
Trial	36
You, Somewhere	38
Melting Rainbow	40
Into Nothingness	42
Water Web	44
Silver Suicide	46
Flooded	48
Escaping Duty	49
Confession Of A Novaturient	51
Teen Travels	53
Solitary Dubiety	55
Pencil To Pen	57
Dangling Dreams	60
Halted Symphony	62
Black Butterflies	63
Empty Stars	65
Wound - Conscience Speaks	67

Within And Without	69
Sunburn	71
Out Of Reach	73
Inky Nights	75
Wordless Wish	77
Together With You	79
Camphor Flames	81
When It Is Spring	82
Prickly Love	83
Do You Know?	85
Timeless Togetherness	87
Handkerchief	89
Nightmares	91
Leaving	93
Here Lies A Human	94
Awakening	96
Thanks To The Fireflies	97
Ahead	99
Some Joy Spared	101
Amaze	102
Towards The Bright Daylight	104
Sentience	106
Happiness - A Tale Of Loss & Longing	108
Creased	109
Acknowledgements	113
Hand Holding	114

STARGAZE

The twinkling stars
in the night sky,
those pretty pearls
strung on an invisible necklace.
The sacred starlight,
that seems to reside
far above the heavens-
in the infinite kingdom
of tranquility.

The ostentatious moon,
proud of her beauty,
smiles serenely
reveling in her own euphoria,
bestowing with magnificent munificence
her holy, enlightening rays.

Together, they are intimidating
arousing queer curiosity in a keen kid
who wonders in awe-
What lies up there?
What secrets to unravel?
What mysteries to unveil?

Engrossed in childish contemplation,
intense imagination,
appealed by the prodigies of nature,
he sets on an innocent, invigorant errand.
An errand of
stargazing...

THROUGH YOUNG EYES

The breeze through my hair,
swirling in the cool morning air;
rivers down the mountain,
clouds 'cross the sky,
all these I savor, as spreading
my wings, I learn to fly.

Taking off is a pain,
landing is a dread,
for through my unkempt feathers
shivers of angst spread.

Crisp autumnal leaves
cake the thoroughfares.
See how my feet dive
into these dusty, crumbling layers!

What sorrows do they hide,
beneath the auburn hue of hearth,
ruefully consoling those barren trees
that dearly lament their dearth?

What elation courses through me
as I skim over the clear waters
whose austere tranquility,
my delirious flight shatters!
Piercing into the pond,
the sunshine proffers me a glance
of those long, weedy kelps
that sway as if in a trance.

Reveling in my newfound skill,
I glide into the night
when the old owl has turned up
to prove its lone hoot's might.
Suddenly, I start feeling uneasy
as if perpetual hopelessness wear on my trail,
The mere thought of it
makes my blood freeze and
my bones go frail.

Thankfully, I find my nest
and its cozy commodity.
I calm my racing heart
amidst the blinding tenebrity-
for now I am safe,
and ready to turn in
'cause there's a new day ahead
to flitter from blue to green to red.

But now I'll rest, dream
about today and how it went by-
teaching, frightening, unveiling and honoring me,
and then, waving goodbye,
all in the blink of an eye.

Now I shut my eyes,
listening to the cricket's cries.
Now I shut my eyes,
to open them at dawn
as the fragrance of the moonflower dies.
Now, I shut my eyes…

WINDOW

I can see it flooding in-
silent, searing light,
blindingly bright;
I am on fire.
The window has enlightened me.

Yesterday,
the storm swept in
and I was all
electrified morale,
electrocuted ideal;
dried by the gale-
drenched again by the rain.
The window had daunted me.

Through its bars,
I can see stars-
melting, dripping starlight
onto roads turned rivers
in a concrete jungle. Then-
leaves whisper a lullaby
and I sleep.
The window thus amazes me.

Seconds. Minutes. Hours.
Millennia altogether.
Myriad souls sit by this window-
witnessing, sensing, believing.
I am here too,
awaiting and forgetting finality.

Hairs may whiten.
Hearts may freeze.
Graves may be dug.
Eulogies and elegies sung.
But the window shall stay-
enlightening, daunting, amazing us,
for a theatre needs curtains
and empty seats, audience.

HIS INSPIRING ENDEAVOURS

He lies far above
concocted in hate and love;
an idol He truly is
and has stupendous strategies
to repel dark forces
He blazes like fiery torches.
Glory and pride
are His bride.
He'll never disgrace-
or with guilt, hide His face.
And with gloom He'll fight
forever, with all His might.
And yet sometimes overpowered
by grey clouds and rain towered.
Despite this ephemeral melancholy
to replenish joy and jolly,
He'll find His way
and it's just to say
He'll bestow with magnanimity
Golden showers with sedulity
He'll strive hard
To the darkness discard
and to spread euphoria,
to repel all phobia.

He'll take the strain
and yet ignore all the pain
till epochal apocalypse He'll burn
and brazenly hold His authority
as venerable,
honorable and formidable;
from Him, there are
infinite things to learn-
From the ever-deserving, never-digressing *sun*.

INVIGORATED ASPIRATIONS

A free bird, I am!
With newfound euphoria,
I flee from servitude,
expecting eternal liberty.

With a sniff of
forthcoming adversities.
I advance with grim premonitions.

Soaring in the turbulent azure,
I wonder-

Who knows? Anytime can a seemingly
tranquil firmament brew
a forbidding tempest!

But I glide…
for I have a future to build…
and in it, mysteries to unravel…

COUNTRYSIDE

Blue all around me.
Blue I can taste.
Breezes whir past me,
kiss my skin with haste.

Green into the horizon.
Green I can see.
Grief is now at bay,
as cuckoos sing for me.

Brown underneath my feet.
Brown lets me live.
Earth caresses my breath,
Earth I can believe.

I heard the call.
When? I cannot recall.
Now I am here,
now I am lost.
Away from heat,
away from frost.

What though I cannot stay?
Though I know I'll bleed when I part—
the countryside, I'll wrap it up
and hide it in my heart.

THE MOONFLOWER'S SMILE

In the still night,
its petals glisten through the dew and
the moonflower grins at me,
as I recite to it
my ecstasy.

Time slips away.
Sunbeams graze the air.
And the moonflower withers.

Now, as I reach euphoria's zenith,
I remember that grin,
that almost
ghostly, ghastly smirk;
that unspoken declaration
of my naïveté, of future's
unpredictable unpredictability.

BLIND

True that I am blind.
True that I cannot see.
But thou orchid in morning sunlight,
why can I not feel thee?
'Tis a pity that I cannot cry
when I am stung by the selfish bee
that in all its sightfulness
couldn't have not hurt me...

BARREN

Now, I hear the breeze
swishing in my pinnae,
tickling out an invisible smile,
inspiring flight while
respiring might.

Eyes dimmed, senses rimmed
as I lay supine,
let the sun shine,
into my black pupils
narrowed by knowledge.

When stars twinkle
and spoons tinkle,
I dream of flocks
cawing, *together*;
cuddling, *together*;

I have tasted elation in me,
deception from them
and again, dejection in me, *alone*.
Draped in poison ivy,
laced with grapevines
I found,
I had aged…

A maroon rose
 of coarse velvet-
shorn of its thorns
clinging to crisp petals,
gone with the gale.

You, my dear
You, my death-
fly me there
where I can write
of victories they care,
and of losses not left bare.

INSIDE

Eyes, you say, are mirrors.
If so, why are mine black?
If inside them stands a canvas,
then why is mine blank?

Yes, stars do shine and
water still flows.
Do you know where?
No, not at night
nor in rivers, but
in the corners of my eyes,
where a quiet tear glows.

And when I smile at you,
lying on meadows, smile with you,
the grass beneath are thorns
        and
my tears take different forms.
I am happy, you are sure,
 aren't you? Why aren't you?

Stay still, and hold my gaze-
you will see a thousand scars.
Behind vision's veil and
my false joyful tale,
you will find a lifeless Mars.

When you look inside,
deep through my painful past
you will finally find me
and I will breathe at last.

Laid bare, I would feel strong
knowing that I wasn't entirely wrong.
And we would be true.
And we would be together.
as weeping and smiling,
we sing an inside song,
sing the inside song…

TRIAL

If I had tried,
could I have saved you?
Could I have quelled the storm?
The dawn had not warned me
that by dusk you will be gone.
The sun had not seen
the eclipse running to him,
or he would have fled,
worn clouds and stayed warm.

Who shall I call my own?
Even tears desert me now.
The sandstorms they cause are
a blissful doom,
for they take me down
to be with you.

Unabashed they roar;
they tell me where I'll be anytime soon.
The tarnished moon still shines.
The air hasn't changed at all.
But the seas are a pinch too salty
and lips, a notch less sweet.
The raindrops defiant, wobble back to the air-
it is the clouds that hastily seek,
yet never again do they meet.

Had I tried,
would you have let me help you?
Would the storm have plucked some other leaf?
Some time,
when the lilies wrinkle and wilt,
the earth will gently kiss their scorched forehead-
and then shall we speak.
Tried and tired,
then shall we speak…

YOU, SOMEWHERE

Did I say that we liked each other?
Did I say that you should have stayed longer?
Now when the clock strikes midnight
and the birds have all flown away-
I dream of you.
I cry for you.
Where are you?
Do you do it too?

The flowers grow ashen.
The ground turns barren
as the sky cracks and falls onto the earth
which now shatters above you
like glass and hearts.
I long for you.
I search for you.
Where have you gone?
Do you do it too?

Liquid roads
on dreary skin that desires your warmth.
Freezing over
to thorny ice before their birth.
My soul has
found another hole.

Come after me.
Come for me,
for I cannot stay
another day, without you.
Do you hear me now?
Do you feel it too?

MELTING RAINBOW

The cold world I am shrouded in,
it shrinks as I shut my eyes.
Suddenly, the air feels too loud
in my expectant ears.
So much so
it makes me want
to flow away, to dissolve in its
supreme sublimity.

My heart is haunted.
My brain, enchanted.
So much for tomorrow,
so less for today!
Dismay has warned me
not to sleep.
But I drift away,
anyway.

Raindrops long for the clouds.
Seeds want back fruits.
No shop in sight.
No leaves murmuring as
I trundle along the
chocolate path of dreams.

What I hold and hanker after
is but a faltering nib, broken-
leaking out its life to shape mine.
My rainbow melts on countless birds
that fly beneath, unfazed.
They look at me through frosted glass,
poor, happy little things.

Would that I could
freeze my tears!
release my fears!
so they could stay with me
> as crystalline yet smudged memory
> as colorful breaths and
> as warm whispers of my melting soul…

INTO NOTHINGNESS

We are carried away
by the fossils of our forefathers
as the wax of time drips duskily
onto graying pastures
where redolent buds blossom
and burgeon
into nothingness.

A lonesome brook trickles nearby,
muddied by its own silt
that it had gloriously eroded
from its once-lush, loam-laden banks
where now stand rotting trunks
of famished, flea-infested trees
staring wistfully
into nothingness.

Vultures scour the ashen skies
and the ravished land beneath
as they too are starving
for what now remains
of formerly flourishing, frolicking fauna
is damned spirits awaiting redemption,
yet fading away silently
into oblivion,
into nothingness.

The twisted tale of this clime
brings back shame-speckled memories
and insipid tears, now that
they have passed away, now that
we have moved on.
Where can we contain,
where must we preserve
these cursed fossils of our forefathers?
Where in the verdant void
should we hide these sacred relics?

So much have we lost!
So much to be found!
With our calamity-conquered consciences,
where will we discover and decipher
these ancient answers
without ourselves giving in
to the Eternal End,
to the luring limbo
Of nothingness ?

WATER WEB

I stand still
clutching the violet sky,
listening to the soothing rhyme
of a gunfire epidemic-
liquid and strategic-
battering the ground.

Citylights set the stage.
The wind kindles and quenches
this godly geometry,
shattered symmetry
before my eyes-
scattered all around.

O water web,
born of distorted light-
who is your prey
hiding in plain sight?
Who were you drawn by
on this monster metal slate?

O water web,
interdimensional vortex-
Will you care enough to
transport me to the realm
of dark beauty
of light revulsion?
I cannot see. I cannot hear.

O water web,
as you vanish from this
charismatic chaos,
will you let me come along?

SILVER SUICIDE

Since when did the world
go black and white?
Hurry! Someone rush out there
and set things right!
For I am bound
in these long, silver chains.
Can no one in this town
come and rid me of my pains?

I'm on a boat, adrift, derelict
and about to sink.
I can't swim and I
threw off the life-vest, I think.
Please, save me, I'm crying;
all alone, I am just scared-
that I'll be dying,
my corpse rotting uncared.

I watch, silent, as the dimmed sun sets
        drowning
into a dark pit that misinterprets.
So I lay down and close my eyes
        shedding
lone tears again as my soul re-despairs.

Should I arise tomorrow again
only to accept defeat?
Or just pass out and hide away
my heart that voids surfeit?

When you find my bones, please
do say a few firm oaths
for the solace of my waning spirit
that still its importance loathes…
that still its impotence loathes…

FLOODED

The dried dandelions in
yonder arid ravine,
surely they didn't hear the roar
of the flood waters gushing.

In but a minute or two,
drowned were the rocks and scorps.
They saw a new world. Of it,
they couldn't see enough!

Underwater frolic.
Who cares for the hell above?
Bubbly prisms everywhere,
a happy time together.

Tomorrow, or a few days hence-
the sun will burn upon us.
What if the flood dries?

Rainbows will vanish. Sand will reign.
Until the sea we cannot see
someday, somehow hears our cries…
someday, somehow heeds our cries…

ESCAPING DUTY

Duty cries: *Come to me.*
I am your home.
I am your destiny.
Does it know of the
lingering melody which
still ripple my eardrums?
For all its might,
and honesty-fenced enclosure,
can duty sense the
bittersweet aftertaste of
hard-earned yet suddenly stolen freedom?

No, it is not sloth
that cloaks me in embracing snugness.
Nor is it phobia.
It is but all those waves
of conscience-crumpling curiosity
crashing onto the shores
of my thirsty knowledge,
of my blooming wisdom,
of my nerve-racking urge
to find it all.

It must be a sin
to escape duty.
But not anybody can snatch
away from me that grin
that awaits
every rueful discovery.

CONFESSIONS OF A NOVATURIENT

Dread, inexplicable dread-
how it creeps into my
mushy rationale,
as I dangle from
the cliff of uncertainty,
about to fall, into
the pit of depravity,
of age's misdirection.

Help? Help seems distant
like the setting sun at the horizon
beyond the churning waters
of rebuke, rebuttal, remonstration.

Letting go appears easy,
but is it right?
The trench beckons me
luring me into impenetrable darkness
where monsters of vice lurk,
threatening to plague
my conscience,
my hard-earned righteousness.

From the grey, glum sky
rains of angst slash and splash
at my shaky, slippery fingers,
tempting me to give up maneuvering,
to give in
to a perennially aberrant course of life.

A sudden streak of lightning
subsumes and divides the sky-
dazing me, teaching me how
a glint of diligence
can enlighten the gloom of amorality.
The adrenaline of optimism
surges through me, and I
thrust myself onto the precipice
inhaling wisps of hope.

As I straighten up
and brush off
the residue of reluctance,
I sense a reassuring warmth.
And I look up to discover
the grim, glum clouds
giving way to

a sun of sincerity,
a tomorrow of tenacity,
a future of fruition…

TEEN TRAVELS

Deep down,
beneath the corpses of long-forsaken hopes
lies my soul
at rest.

Up above,
beyond the sprawling skies of pleasant thoughts
waits patiently
my aim.

Steep climb.
Crowded mind.
How can I not fall?
And
if I trip-
perchance, lose my grip,
who'll answer my distress call?

Yet ahead I march-
I try to live up.
Eyes shut
knees buckle,
but I do not give up.

At night
when I sleep,
calming my tired soul,
I dream of life
and how it'd be
when I reach my goal,
when I reach my goal,
when I reach my goal…

SOLITARY DUBIETY

Why is it so?
Why are the streets empty?
It's hard to accept
and my doubts are plenty.

There are no more children;
only there phantasms remain.
Their bicycles rot in the garage,
and the hopes for fun are slain.

The racquet stays isolated,
with other accessories bound.
The shuttle cock? Oh! Don't ask,
it's nowhere to be found.

The chuckles of our craic
do not resonate anymore,
through the eerily deserted lanes
analogous to a secluded shore.

Where are those times,
when we ran and played
till the soles of our slippers
were all but torn and frayed?!

Do tell me, is this fair?
That imprisoned in Cells,
we never our
 ecstasies and dolours share?

Do tell me, should this continue?
To fixate oneself on
Visions and Tops,
is this okay with you?

Should I not yearn
to relive these memories?
Or should I just slump back,
only to stare at mental fripperies?

Will those good ol' days return?
Will the shriveled
ebullience regrow?
Dumbstruck by this
plethora of conundrums,
My heart longingly asks-
Why is it so?

PENCIL TO PEN

I held a pencil
in my tiny trembling hands,
drew lines, letters and learned to live.
I held a pencil,
fearing it was too sharp,
or maybe too blunt
to impress Ma'am with a flawless homework.
I held a pencil and began sketching
the vivid yet unclear image of my dream
onto white pages of countless notebooks.

They were but insipid
contrasted to
ravishing, raging red of the teacher's pen.
And yet they blushed
when embraced by a rare "Good".

Often it broke, my pencil.
Even the infamous "cutter" was rude at times.
How I longed then
to grab an unsophisticated pen,
to get rid of this fussy pencil-
arrogant, impulsive, erratic.

Now that
ink spots stain my palms
and aching, twisted fingers,
the pencil with the broken nib
is my only nightmare,
and my only fond guilt.

I never now forget to
feel its warm comfort in my
callused hands.

I try now to forget my
silly misgivings and thoughtless begrudgings
about my pencil that is now
long lost, long sacrificed to
the concrete commandments of my pen-

insensitive, indelible, indispensable.

Only tears can smudge this ink.
But they too are hesitant to fall-
Who shall pick them up in loving care
and caress away their crushing despair?

So when I now hold a pencil,
it speaks to my silent reproach.
It scorns me for having scorned it
But it knows, and
I know too that

I left behind some part of me
on that cold cliff where
childhood perched alive,
when I began my slow unsteady steps
on a lone, ancient bridge

to remorseful remembrance,
to lifeless labor,
to melancholic maturity.

DANGLING DREAMS

My dreams hang from yonder oak tree.
They are old, yet not old enough.
They have shut their ears to the
whistling wind that whispers *Life is rough.*

My dreams are autumn leaves.
They are sad but not without hope.
Like snow in melting winter,
with fate, they dream to elope.

They are in search of a home
that never was, yet is long-lost.
They look for a warm memory
that they can put on free of cost.

Where is the sun? they think.
They cannot yet brave the dark.
Still they weave tapestries of truth.
They dream to leave their mark.

They cannot stand the listless nights
shrouded in mist and dust.
In their fitful sleeps they fail to know,
the dying fire betrays their trust.

My dreams are ill from being alone
yet they have to survive, they know.
Some love and daylight would them good
so that I dream more and grow.

HALTED SYMPHONY

Sole, solemn moments in the dark
when all is asleep...
we see the mirror
and the blunt, gentle thorns behind.

Humanity is a tendency,
a cool, sublime vapor-
it trickles down my spine
it is all a game of staying kind.

Whispers to the soul,
blown off course, of course
like a moth with broken wings...
Who did hear it cry?

On a distant hill where
the sun singes the lake,
echo my haunted wails;
I remember the *Why*.

Halted symphony in space
where time stretches out with thoughts apace,
Will you recall me in your dreams?
Hear my screams? Hear my screams?

BLACK BUTTERFLIES

Infernos of insecurity blaze.
Hammers of hubris pound.
Sparks of sleaze spread.
And thus, the faculty's factory
fabricates Its eggs.

Like an outbreak
they crawl and eat away
verity's vegetation.
Miniature monsters
poking pits through
a vain, venous heart;
Now reign The larvae.

Enough growth!
Needed anon is thought.
Deep, dark contemplation
within a creative cocoon;
perceiving, processing, pondering,
plotting their way in
a placid, putrid pupa.

Arrival of auspice.
Departure of delay.

Now they will soar
into thunderous tenebrity,
flapping wings of shadow
that but the sunlight slay.

That soul, then, shall leap
from a cliff unthinkably steep
that the world in
awe shall see
deceived by, and beneath, its glee…

as in wide, white skies
flutter black butterflies…

EMPTY STARS

We are now
in another dimension.
Where there is no sun,
but where the darkness burns.
Where nights are white,
where moons are black,
Now, we are empty stars.

Here, we see you, bared,
as what you truly are- HumAnimals.
No, we didn't see the light.
No, we didn't breathe our life.
You remember us not, yet we aren't dead.
Here, we are empty stars.

Here, we hear you, everywhere,
as what you really are- KillIngrates.
Invert the night's hues.
See the white as black.
We'll be there, draped in the dark.
Watching you restlessly at rest,
as empty stars.

Who is to blame? Tell us,
for we didn't sense it.
No, we couldn't know it.
We were destined for doom,
decided dead in her womb.
We are empty stars.

Who tried to save us?
She tried to save us.
Did she? Could she?
No use now.
We are empty stars.

WOUND- CONSCIENCE SPEAKS

Bone. Flesh. Blood.
Sparks of pain with the
glee of security.
A battleground, a holocaust.
In a wound, 's there only
bone, flesh, blood?

Guillotined? Hanged? Burnt alive?
Physically, yes. Mentally, also yes.
No latibule, is there?
When you reach the other end,
they'll ask- Were you
guillotined? hanged? burnt alive?

Time. Care. Patience.
Prerequisites not procured.
What do they go for?
Where are they selling?
With no one around,
how will you find
time? care? patience?

Remorse! Regret! Repentance!
Where were they till now?
You're being watched.
your misdeeds with censure attached.
Gloom's gone. Ecstasy's extinct.
For you, life is naught but
remorse! regret! repentance!

You're over it now.
Now, you will move on.
But your wound shall stare, agape.
Oozing out shame's pus,
stinking of flawed ideals-
a black hole decorating
the tattered tapestry of
your damned, doomed soul.

I am eternal.
So is your wound:
a souvenir of sorrow
a memoir of misery,
one amongst myriads in your
perished past...
putrescent present...
festerous future...

WITHIN AND WITHOUT

There is turbulence within
and esperance without.
Everybody smiles and laughs
while in scarcity,
their souls shriek and shout.

They water their flowerbeds,
grow thorns and prick fingers.
Then they drink the blood, for
of sanctity they are harbingers.

They hold hands and
bimble down deserted lanes.
But the sky weeps in glum empathy
as they silently rot with their pains.

When they talk, songs pour out
like the melody of drizzle
on parched earth.
In sooth, they are but burning alive as
together, they warm themselves
by the hearth.

They dread that there will never be
short-lived but some shared glee.

Would it hurt to stay behind
and caress some hair,
while they let the black clouds burst,
and wail in dwindling despair?

Would it kill to speak up
softly in their ears,
that they'll stay and stand by
through chaotic days, months and years?

Perhaps then there will be
short-lived but some shared glee.

Esperance within;
Turbulence without.
Their souls shall smile and laugh while
in jollity, they shriek and shout.

SUNBURN

Glad was the sun that
the mist was gone, that
the clouds were sparse
through the airy marsh.
I knew this for I loved the sun.

It was a pure love,
I was a dauntless dove-
scorched by heated affection
         yet
seduced by blinding reflection.
Yes, I knew that I loved the sun.

Alas! I went too far,
delved in a flaming war.
Too close, I lost my sight;
too far, I see no light.
I doubt that I ever loved the sun.

When I came, he should have known.
He glared instead, ablaze he shone.
I flew higher;
      I was mad in love. But
set aflame and fused,
      I could never evolve.
Why, I knew I never loved the sun!

Now that I have had some time
I find my life a wasteful rhyme.
The sun was, after all, a star-
brilliant, but better off when far.

But I was daring
        and so dumb,
the sun I couldn't possibly numb.
Now that I'm hardened,
        charred and tough,
I know I didn't love the sun enough.
No, I didn't love the sun enough…

OUT OF REACH

No man has ever spoken
of the fairy who lives by the brook.
No child has ever dreamt
of stealing her great wings.
She is out of reach
of hungry hooligans. Would that
she came out! Or better still,
if she ceased to be!
A hearth amidst a springtime blizzard,
She is, in a steaming desert, an unreal mirage.
I did but hear her once
at eventide, in sylvan solitude
through distant birdsongs.
She was singing
to the dying sun,
to the maroon moon and
to the fathomless space between them.
She was singing
of unnamed winds whose
coy courtships made her blush,
of uncharted waters that
smoothed her rebellious feathers.

I turned toward the voice
and saw but void and vain hope.
Perhaps it's for the best
that she chooses seclusion.
For all I know,
she is only out of reach
that I may someday find her,
that she may, till then
woo and vex me
with subtle spells of surreal separation.

INKY NIGHTS

On my desk, my ransacked, holy workplace
I had left a note- for you to read.
Somewhere near its bottom left corner,
there's a smudged word,
blurred in a mildly condescending fashion
like wind-smoothed walk tracks in a desert.

It had great many letters, of different colors.
They had deluged onto the silken, vanilla sheet
as monsoon-released floodgates. They were
dead leaves that clenched their crisp axils
but were slapped away by a mere breeze.

Beside the note was a pen, perhaps left uncapped
by a quivering hand, exsanguinated and sated.
The pen must have waited for you
amid the slovenly stacks of discarded pages.
It must have inhaled their sad scent, and
then died, flowed into the Invisible with time. Gone.

I remember the lamp's coughing glow-
dwindling, demanding to be seen, sadistic yet sympathetic.
It was inanimate, but greened my eyes still.

Perhaps this was all a dream, a happy one, but
too bad- the sun couldn't bear my fantasy,
for I now wear night, my dimly sparkling cloak.
I wish I could carry the note with me
as all it does on the table is rot and fade.

You never came; my heart twitched and twisted,
spewed blood, went white.
But when you depart, I pray, wear the moonlight night,
for the stars damned cannot touch the moon
but they know she is there…
and they burn on till dawn…

WORDLESS WISH

we had sat
in the bursting bush.
the earth in our noses,
crickets in our ears,
stars in our eyes
up above.

then when a star
went streaking across
the pearly midnight paradise,
I saw it
but did not let you.

did you hear
the river yonder, being
the traitor that she was,
as she giggled
at my fancy?

the zealous gusts
of flowery zephyrs though,
they didn't pass you
subtle, scented hints that-

that night, when
the sun slept and
of spring he dreamt,
I had wished alone.
I alone had wished.
and I had wished
for you…

TOGETHER WITH YOU

Together with you,
what things I could do!
Only there are seven seas betwixt us,
and savage wilderness beyond.
Yet I can't stop wondering,
how blessed I'd be!
It would be so true,
if only I could be
together with you.

There'd be so much joy.
Spring would be brighter and fuller still.
Even winter frost would be welcome
were we to lie on that grassy hill.
You'd hum songs and I'd cry.
When you laugh, I'd just sit by
and watch you till I sleep.
From the cliff of fantasy will I leap
and remember with stabs of truth
that the moon is but still without hue
as I was not, am not, perhaps will never be,
together with you.

The night before, I had a dream.
I was mad in desolation.
You hid in the shadows
awaiting liberation.
Fortune slyly smirked but anon relented.
You emerged blithe,
in gelid sunlight you bathed.
Thus I dreamed of emeralds,
rubies and gems galore that I'd accrue
now that I finally was
together with you.

But 'twas fleeting and chimerical
you were still out of reach.
Today
I'm on my way
on this murky mutiny,
intent on thwarting destiny.
I might fail, or sip sweet success.
I'd lose nothing and gain all
if only fate I could undo
and in undying utopia, reside
together with you...
together with you...

CAMPHOR FLAMES

Suddenly it came to life
and calcined away my candid dreams.
A gunshot, deadly and feathery.
The camphor flames charred my eyes.
When they blew, away the flew,
having charged the supine skies.

I had created it. It's a shame-
for long had it cooled my fervor-fired palms,
and yet I had stayed graceless and lame.
When I cried, it wafted out to me,
caressed my trachea, said nothing.
How could I thank it?
'Twas already a memory.

These camphor flames, dear and deceptive-
dark is their fitful heart
but none so much as your loving warmth.
They could never have crossed the length
of their sweet, sordid scent
as I now gather in their death,
lost in fleeting fumes
of faithless fancy…..

WHEN IT IS SPRING

Snow falls like silken feathers
around me.
I sip warm water and smile
in winter frost
lost in silent thought.

Leaves re-grow and shine green;
yellowed yesterday, yet they dance
all the same
with the rose-tinted wind
in whispering melody
in harlequin harmony.

I am hungry for tomorrow.
I have glued together cracked glass.
It is a steady breath
that I now sense–
now that it is spring.
It is a painful peace
that I now wear–
now that the air is blossoming,
now that I am me.

Where does a circle start?
Where does it end?
Infinite flowers on an endless fence
where do they blend?

PRICKLY LOVE

Prickly love.
No antidote
for its subtle scalds.
No better bliss
than its kiss of compathy.

Hand in hand,
arguing like
competing crows.
Strolling along the shore
as the sky cries
as the sun cringes.
Barefoot,
pebbles underneath.
You smile, and
they are suddenly petals.

Sitting alongside
on a cold bench,
sipping coffee
humming unmusically.
When our eyes meet,
cacophony ceases,
blooms into an effluence
of heavenly harmony.

What would I do
without your glares and glee?
Lost in oceans of murk, perhaps.
No light to warm me,
no hand to hold,
to trawl me back above.

Dear, what would I be,
without your
prickly love?

DO YOU KNOW?

Do you know?
Do you know what it takes
to gift a serendipitous smile
to a dreadful human?

Do you know?
Do you know how it feels
when one is
betrayed by a kin,
who has disguised themselves
by gilding poison with fake affection?

Do you know
what it is, to be
ostracized, to be opposed and oppressed,
to coercively be a recluse?

Do you know
the ineffable pain
when one endures
the sorrow of lovelessness?

And after all this,
do you know
what it takes
to mend the bond-
infected with vices
infested with inadvertent amorality?

Do you know how
to restore a
dismayed, strained relationship,
to retie the rended, long-broken
yet once-unbreakable
thread of consanguinity?

If one is willing to bestow;
if one is prepared
to set aside ego;
if one tries to
revive the former ecstasy;

If one is impartial enough-
all it takes,
is but an ubiquitous yet rare,
affordable yet priceless entity;
all it takes
is pure, unadulterated love.

TIMELESS TOGETHERNESS

We met under the sequoia tree
yearning to shrug and look away
and failing,
but failing,
yet failing…

The wind danced through the trees;
your hair played with it too.
And the sun shaded your eyes
and the bewitching enigmas within.

How we soared in celestial ecstasies
while rooted in the earth's bosom!
How delirious were our senses
amid newfound love's germination!

Nature stood witness as
we stepped into
the boat of togetherness.
And so began our odyssey
across the sea of life.

Now, at the other shore
when the end inches closer
and frayed is the fabric of age-
our memories remain lively, untainted.

One last shared
remembrance of requitement that
we met
under the sequoia tree...

HANDKERCHIEF

Now flash before me
those intimate moments we shared,
as I glance at
these intricate patterns on
your handkerchief...

The perfume of memories
wafts through my senses
as I hold
this heartwarming yet heartrending
cloth, that is,
your handkerchief...

How shall I speak?
Who shall I share with?
the joy our togetherness,
the grief of our separation and
all those thoughts that
pluck and prick my heartstrings,
as I daydream while
prizing this discovery of
your handkerchief…

Should I not be envious,
that this cloth that
in your pocket resided has
withstood while I,
who housed your heart, have
withered
since our parting?

Draping my bosom
with this cloth,
I sigh and I shiver
and I smile. Yes, I smile.
I smile as a tear
breaks the dam of my reserve
and sedately slithering down
wets my parched heart,
wets my famished soul,
wets
your handkerchief…

NIGHTMARES

The memory of that
which could not be held
in hands, warm and wet;
in tears, silent-
it wakes in my mind with a scream.

Nightmares are peaceful,
'tis the heart that shudders.
It is deafened by its own shrieks.
Nightmares are hopeful,
'tis the mind that plays the devil.
It murders the blossoming buds
with its somber somersaults.

How shall I heal these wounds,
these scars that I proudly wear?
For they have become me.
And I, them.
We are warriors in the dead of night.
Whom do we fight?
Whom do we save?
Whose blood is spilt?
Where does it go?

Nightmares are beautiful.
They are paramours in glorious union.
Reveries, we forget.
But nightmares are never hurtful;
they live on in daylight.
They wait in patient posture,
after torture, in merciful respite.

Their tree forever grows,
drinks blood; its flowers glisten white
'gainst the black of its twisted boughs
that have ensnared many a kite…

LEAVING

Couldn't you see the pain in my eyes?
My agonized winces as I stifled my cries?
You crucified me and I happily bled.
Why couldn't you, dear, for once understand-
you were rotting me into thewless sand?

No doubt I'm dying to yell and scream
as I run from your demons in my dream,
but I lay quiet, quivering, beside you, love.
How I yearn for your fingers through my hair!
For your company, compathy and affectionate care!

Perhaps you don't know that I too feel.
And that low blows take time to heal;
you are dearly drunken in scented spring.
Or perhaps I'm going paranoid or worse-
I cannot comprehend your endearment's course.

I bet it's time for me to leave,
for you, beloved, you make me grieve
in grey shadows beneath silent smiles.
I bet it's time for me to go.
But I love you,
so I'll go slow…

HERE LIES A HUMAN

when the time comes-

tilt your head and
close your eyes and
hear the clouds slide

in a sky blue black white
on a day not dim nor bright
hear the sun hide

thunder minus sound
lightning minus light
think of your doom
on a pouring starry night

when the clouds dissolve
open your eyes and
see the light

there is no above
although your stopped heart aches
walk into your sight

here you will lie
for you are, or were, a human
when the time comes-

tears in your eyes
let them not fall
there is no ground
you are too tall.

AWAKENING

When the mist
touched my lips
my eyes watered at its love.
Two steps, and
      I flew away.

The shrieks of the wind
made my ears bleed.
Sun, the pitiful sage-
it blinded me, so
      I would not see.

In the dark,
      as I trembled
I heard a song from below.
My legs felt so weak
and the tune made me sleep.

Was it a reverie,
or a moonlit dream?
It was there that I awoke next;
there I met me.
And never again since then
have I ever turned in.

THANKS TO THE FIREFLIES

Fireflies
in the pond of my heart
where weeds entangle laughter
and kelps ensnare joy
while some blackness sets them apart,
away from the fireflies
in the pond of my heart.

A boat too large it sinks.
A ship too light it sways,
in the waves unnatural
in my heart's pond-
that which resides beyond
the land where no fireflies
can kindle some art
in the blue-black pond of my heart.

That prehistoric flood which
had boiled away the sun
from inside of me and my blood-
it is now on fire, and I'm glowing too
as I let the fireflies pierce and dart
about the deep, dark pond of my heart.

These are alien insects
for what fly there is that in water gambols?
Not that my heart is earthly-
jovian scales, lunar waters, martian fish, solar scarcity
and what not!

Who knew that fireflies from the multiverse
would in my soul intersperse
and the null their frolic would cause
would clear this putrid marsh?
And that new lilies would bloom,
shine violet 'neath a whitewashed moon
as I at last rest and from sorrow part
thanks to the fireflies in the
pure pond of my heart.

AHEAD

I am
freed from memories
spiraling miracles unseen.
It was dark when I lost my way,
through the black and invisible thorns
        I saw the day...

Crawling along the shore,
I am broken by sweat and salt.
My hair with the gale betrays me
        and flits back
but the solemn sea gifts me a new path,
        so I do not halt...

I never knew time crept slower at night
and I weep in the shadows of the past.
Cold, I wrap myself in a shawl of grief.
O that the stars were closer, shining me
        warm, white relief!

Could I have known that I would move on?
Could love have shown that I wasn't alone?

I saw the moon dragging
along a diamond-strewn road.
I saw the sun pushing away
night from its nightly abode.

I breathed
as I felt my shawl evaporate.
Something had let me glow;
ahead, it had let me flow-
>to journeys beyond.
>Life was every second.

SOME JOY SPARED

Smelling, savoring wet dust,
plummeting down the sky;
wingless,
yet attempting to fly.
I could have caught hold
          of some doubt
from the tree of misery.

Noisily breathless,
watching the mad life beneath
weightless as a rose,
          landing peacefully
on the listless, lonely lake
          of placidity.

White around me,
I inhale purity-
a sad, humble truth
a virtue-mottled verity
and some joy spared
on the crammed, crumpled sheet
where my heart draws life
with blood
thick, tortuous but true.

AMAZE

Yes, you are breathing.
Why, you are alive!
But drying is fantasy's ocean
where, naked, once you dived.

Days are days and nights are nights
Butterflies are moths- mere insects.
But facts are a sore smokescreen
that your soul has worn ,
and a fuel that feeds your defects.

Dust, soot, smoke you inhale and die.
Your brain is by friction worn out.
Though the ground is wet, your feet are burnt-
from these acids no seeds ever sprout.

You need to go back.
Through calm chaos,
you need to paint
those specks of imagination
that with dreamless days grow faint.

You need to see.
Through calm chaos,
you need to believe
ere trees turn black and from
contrite crimes there is no reprieve.

Home is not far, so trudge along.
Feel what you see and sing a song.
Enter a maze, but don't be fazed.
Retrace your path and be amazed.

And when the factory is on fire
and the heavens shoot rain-
night shall be day, butterflies will from moths differ
and you will be whole again.
You will be one again.

TOWARDS THE BRIGHT DAYLIGHT

At the stroke of the midnight hour
halted breaths fill the air.
A joy blooms in the waiting hearts
of us Indians, as lotuses for the sunrise prepare.

All eyes do water as the fiery sun
lights the tricolor, unfurled in glory.
All souls do rejoice as drowned in
the anthem's symphony, they recall its story.

They say they taste freedom,
we hear orations in streets and halls
of million hands that drew
our nation out of its wretched thralls.

Memories re-spun as telling tapestries;
homage sung to the soil
are all but fleeting, futile
if we at all are loath to toil.

The scent of liberation that
we think we inhale,
it wafts from its mother Conscience
that is close to turning stale.

Pledge. Vow. Oath. Mere words -
precarious, treacherous.
The light can burn bright
only when amid hurricanes of hindrance,
ahead, we trudge;
when infernos scorch us
yet we do not budge;
when the nation is our deck,
our minds, the dreamers,
and pure hearts, their supreme judge.

SENTIENCE

Sentience: it lay
shivering, stuttering inside
evolution's hatching egg.
It was scared, hopeful,
reluctant and curious all the same.
Where had it been till now?
Like a mother's caress
light kissed its eyes,
and sentience awoke.

Where was it? What was this place?
For the first time,
it smelt the fresh fragrance
of the misty morning.
For the first time,
it heard the leaves sighing,
the river gushing and
its heart thudding
inside a new, healthy ribcage.

But how had it come into being?
It needed to kiss its gratitude
onto its still-unknown creator,
for this world was wondrous

and sentience itself was beautiful still.
Yet suddenly it sensed hunger-
for what? It didn't know.

It looked around, tense.
It took a step forward, then back,
Lone tears spilled from
ignorantly luminous eyes.
And sentience slept.

Only sentience knows
what it dreamt of.
Not of hunger, not of its mother, no.
Perhaps, it sought wisdom,
yet was loath to let go
of the soothing shadows.
Perhaps, it desired freedom:
wings to carry him
toward the untrodden paths of the future.

Or perhaps,
it didn't dream at all.
Who could blame it?
Sentience had only just been born.
It had much to know.
It had much to learn…

HAPPINESS-
a tale of loss and longing

Do you remember that day,
when we had sat together on peace's bay?
You, my mavourneen, were all but beatific,
I, a comrade, by your allure, rendered static!

Those waters of wonder, splashed at my feet,
washing away all my memories;
and from life we did purloin several joyous stories.
I implored, *"Cling to me, dear, please don't flee,*
Your dearth will bereave me of all glee!"

But not a word escaped your lips
as you smiled your way to fading memory.
And there I was, alone,
abandoned to unending misery.

So, I leaped into that ocean,
plunging deeper and deeper
wishing you would trawl me back
before faith gave way,
before trust gave up,
before I gave in
to eternal stupor...

CREASED

A bud with creased edges,
amid some forgotten pledges.

Some flaws there be in life's painted pouches,
that do make us whole in our muffled ouch's.

Unwittingly paining the one we love most
like the ocean eroding her companion coast.

If the bees were time, I'm sure they wouldn't mind
draining away life's nectar, leaving no drops behind.

So why cry as you sip the bittersweet tea
of life's sugary, salty, bland, sour (in)consistency?

O mirth, we woo you, "Beloved, be my crown;
My door is ajar, come in, be my clown!"

O dearth, we shoo you, but you find your way in.
It's no use, we know; we let you sleep on our skin.

What is life? Tell me- some blood and a heart?
An irony? Mirage? Or a wounded skylark?

Tethered, wrinkled, but the truth is this-
As we all have known, know or will know that life is-

A bud with creased edges,
amid some forgotten pledges.

Some flaws there be in life's painted pouches,
that but make us whole in our muffled ouch's.

ACKNOWLEDGEMENTS

Even amidst the tumults and turmoils of worldly existence, there is always something that a person can be thankful for. For me, there is an entire universe to thank.

I can never be grateful enough:

to my parents, who gave me being and purpose, who love me in the simplest way there is and who have let me bloom like a humble flower on a verdant riverbank.

to my teachers- every single one of them- for helping me look into myself, for letting me discover myself through their eyes and emotions and for teaching me the difference between a well-educated and a well-formed mind.

to my friends, with whom I have grown to admire the nuanced beauty of companionship, who have, without knowing it themselves, urged me to realize what it is to be human.

finally, to that unseen force of instinct and art, that divine intervention, which has given wings to my thoughts and which, I hope, will live on forever, making this world a better place- a better home for humanity.

HAND HOLDING

Tears come to our eyes
when we see
your innocent eyes
      searching for words and ideas,
              always novel…
your calm and pure mind
      ripples with serene thought…
you sail kites of your imagination
           in the deep blue sky…

When we see you writing poems
to express your emotions and feelings fluent
              as a tiny astronaut,
you wander in the sky of vast creativity
with a sensible heart and innovative mind…

Dear son,

The journey of creativity is never easy,
        not always pleasant…
with both pleasurable pain and painful pleasure,
sometimes it is like
        the blooming of a fragrant flower…
        seldom a snake eating its own tail…

Our joy knows no bounds...
when we see you
     stepping on the pious path of poetry.

With all our affection and heartfelt wishes...

We pray the Almighty
to shower upon you His blessings.
May you swim with success
         to earn the lilies and lotuses
          from the ponds of poetry.....

The most valuable gift in our lives, our son.

                        Your loving parents,

                        Dr. Nibedita
                        Dr. Dinabandhu

www.ingramcontent.com/pod-product-compliance
Lightning Source LLC
Chambersburg PA
CBHW031124080526
44587CB00011B/1108